MW00637581

Comfort Food

gets a **vegan** makeover

Photographs and Design by Jason Lugo

Printed in Canada

www.jillskeem.com

ISBN-10: 0988658801
ISBN-13: 978-0-9886588-0-6

Dedication

“I would like to thank my husband, Tom, for his constant love, support, patience, and willingness to taste anything. But more importantly, his honesty in expressing his likes and dislikes!”

"A special thanks to Jason Lugo, this cookbook would never have happened without him."

Introduction

Comfort Food Gets a Vegan Makeover is for those who want to add healthier meals to their diet, who are or want to become vegetarian, who have vegetarians coming to dinner or who are practicing Meatless Mondays. So, basically this cookbook is for everyone!

Today, every cooking show, magazine recipe and celebrity chef mentions Comfort Food. It's everywhere! *Comfort Food Gets a Vegan Makeover* is a compilation of traditional comfort foods made over using plant-based, wholesome ingredients and *real food*.

These recipes are comforting and delicious! This cookbook proves that comfort food can be tasty, healthy and quick.

Comfort Food Gets a Vegan Makeover will allow you to still have the comfort food experience, but without the guilt and more importantly, the angioplasty.

So, give these recipes a try and hopefully you will enjoy them as much as my family and friends. Who knows, when you think of comfort food, perhaps these dishes will become your new favorites.

Categories

11

19

33

53

67

89

111

131

Glossary

Barley Malt: A sweetener made from sprouted barley that is cooked into a sweet syrup.

Brown Rice Syrup: Thick, light-brown sweetener similar to honey, made by fermenting brown rice. It also comes in a powdered form.

Kuzu Root Starch: A white starch powder made from the root of the wild mountain kuzu plant. It also grows in the south and is known as "kudzu". Used as a thickener for sauces, gravies, puddings and soups.

Sea Salt: An unrefined salt obtained from evaporated sea water. It may be sun-dried or baked in a kiln and contains no added chemicals such as iodine, sugar or other additives.

Seitan: It is wheat gluten and commonly referred to as "wheat meat". It is a great source of protein and is very popular as a meat substitute.

Soy Sauce: When I list the ingredient, soy sauce, in my recipes, I use Johsen's organic shoyu. It is a traditional Japanese soy sauce that is fermented and still alive. You can use regular soy sauce, just make sure it is organic. If you are gluten-intolerant, use the organic Tamari soy sauce.

Tempeh: A fermented soybean product used in sandwiches to salads to stews.

Vegenaise®: A non-dairy, egg-free product made from soy with the same texture and taste similar to Miracle Whip®.

"Whenever I use the term "blend" in my soup recipes, I use a hand-held immersion blender, but you can use a regular blender."

"Many of the products I use can now be found in grocery and natural food stores."

"When deep frying, you can reuse the same oil 2-3 times. Just store it in a glass jar or keep in a covered pot."

"I list canned beans in my recipes for convenience, but you can always use homemade beans in the same quantity."

Table of Contents

Breakfast

Appetizers

Soups

Sandwiches

Main Courses

Side Dishes

Salads

Desserts

pg. 80

Breakfast

Baked Oatmeal

A friend made this dish for me on a cold, winter morning and I thought it was delicious. Turns out, it was from her son-in-law who was from Wisconsin. The original recipe had a lot of sugar, so I made a few alterations to make it healthier.

Ingredients:

Serves 8

4 cups steel-cut oats
8 cups soymilk
1 tsp. almond extract
¼ cup maple syrup
2 cups dried cherries
2 large apples, unpeeled & grated
1 cup sliced almonds, toasted
sea salt (1 pinch per 1 cup of oats)
safflower oil

Method:

1. Preheat oven to 400º.
2. Mix everything together except almonds and put in a large greased Dutch oven.
3. Cover and bake for at least one hour.
4. Stir often to prevent oats from sticking and to become creamy in consistency.
5. Stir in almonds before serving or use them as a garnish.

Raisins, dried apricots, or other dried fruit can be used.

French Toast

I love French toast and wanted to make it healthier. This might become your Sunday morning favorite.

Ingredients:

Serves 4

8 slices of sourdough bread
4 cups soy, almond or rice milk
1 tsp. cinnamon
1/4 tsp. sea salt
1 tsp. vanilla extract
safflower or vegetable oil

Method:

1. Whisk soy milk, cinnamon, sea salt and vanilla extract together in a large, flat bowl.

2. Dip bread in mixture on both sides. Let soak a few seconds on each side.

3. Heat a little safflower oil on a griddle or skillet and fry on each side until golden brown.

Serve with maple syrup or heat up brown rice syrup in a saucepan with a dash of cinnamon

Tofu "Egg" Scramble

Often times, I sauté whatever leftover veggies I have to make this dish. So don't feel limited by this recipe. Tofu scramble can be a breakfast or lunch dish. Just let it cool down, put in a wrap and you have a tasty sandwich.

Ingredients:

Serves 4

1 16oz. block tofu, extra-firm
1/2 cup onion, diced
1/2 cup mushrooms, sliced
1/2 tsp. curry powder or turmeric
1/8 cup water
sea salt
soy sauce
olive or sesame oil
1/4 cup scallion, sliced for garnish

Method:

1. Heat 1 Tbsp. oil in skillet, sauté onions 1-2 minutes with a pinch of sea salt until translucent.
2. Add mushrooms, sauté 1-2 minutes. Break up tofu into skillet. Add turmeric and/or curry powder. Sauté together.
3. Add water, stir, cover and simmer 5 minutes.
4. Add 1/2-1 tsp. soy sauce. Cover and let cook 5 minutes.
5. If you would like to add any frozen vegetables, add them now with a pinch of sea salt.
6. Garnish with scallion.

Appetizers

Beer-Battered Green Beans

Middle Eastern Hummus

Vegetable Egg Rolls

Vegetable Tempura

Sassy Salsa

Game Day Bean Dip

Homemade Tortilla Chips

Seitan "Steak" Fingers

Beer-Battered Green Beans

I bought green beans at the farmer's market and thought they would make a yummy battered and deep fried appetizer. Although, what wouldn't!

Ingredients:

Serves 4

1 lb. fresh green beans
(trimmed & patted dry)
1 cup unbleached white flour
1/2 tsp. sea salt
1/4 tsp. black pepper
1 tsp. oregano
1/2 chili powder (optional)
1 can beer, tonic or sparkling water
safflower oil
paper towels

Method:

1. Whisk dry ingredients together and slowl add beer until consistency is like pancake batter.
2. Heat 5 inches of oil in large Dutch oven. To test if oil is hot enough, drop a dab of batter into it, if it hits the bottom and bounces up quickly, oil is ready.
3. Dip green beans into batter and fry until golden brown.
4. Remove from oil and drain on paper towel.
5. Sprinkle lightly with sea salt.

Substitute onions, mushrooms, or other vegetable instead of green beans.

Middle Eastern Hummus

This authentic Syrian hummus recipe can be used as an appetizer, snack or sandwich. To make different flavors, omit coriander, cumin and paprika and add either olives, red peppers, roasted garlic or any other flavors you prefer.

Ingredients:

Serves 6

1 15oz. can garbanzo beans
2 Tbsp. tahini paste
1/4 cup lemon juice, freshly squeezed (Approx. 1-2 lemons)
1/2 tsp. ground coriander
1/2 tsp. cumin
1/2 tsp. paprika
1/4 tsp. sea salt
cayenne pepper or paprika for garnish
olive oil
pine nuts, toasted

Method:

1. Open can of garbanzo beans and reserve liquid.
2. Mix garbanzo beans, tahini, lemon juice, spices and salt in either a blender or food processor.
3. Gradually add bean liquid to achieve desired consistency.
4. Chill at least 1/2 hour prior to serving.
5. Drizzle 1-2 Tbsps. oil on top and sprinkle with either cayenne pepper or paprika.
6. Garnish with pine nuts.

Vegetable Egg Rolls

I grew up eating Chinese food almost every Sunday night. Ordering egg rolls was a must! Today, many restaurants do not offer vegetable egg rolls, but now you can make your own

Ingredients:

Serves 4

4 egg roll wrappers
1/2 cup onion, thinly sliced half moons
1 cup cabbage, finely sliced
1/4 cup carrots, thin matchsticks
1 Tbsp. cilantro, finely sliced
sea salt
sesame seed oil
safflower oil
paper towels

Dipping Sauce Ingredients:

4 Tbsp. soy sauce
1 Tbsp. stone ground mustard
3/4 cup water
1/4 tsp. ginger juice, freshly grated
1 scallion, finely sliced

Egg Roll Method:

1 Heat 1 Tbsp. sesame oil in skillet, sauté onions with pinch of sea salt.

2 Add cabbage, sauté 1-2 minutes and then carrots Sauté until vegetables are slightly soft. Transfer to a bowl and mix in cilantro. Let mixture cool.

3 When cool, place egg roll wrapper on diagonal, scoop 1 Tbsp. vegetable mixture in middle.

4 Fold bottom up and over vegetables. Wet sides of wrapper with water using fingers. Fold sides in and over first flap. Wet edge of bottom flap and roll to close.

5 Heat 5 inches of oil to 350° in Dutch oven, deep fry egg roll until golden brown. Place on paper towel to absorb excess oil.

Dipping Sauce Method:

1 Place soy sauce, mustard and water in saucepan.

2 Gently heat and stir until mustard is dissolved.

3 Grate ginger and squeeze juice using fingers into saucepan. Add scallions, stir thoroughly.

Vegetable Tempura

Tempura is so satisfying when you are craving something rich and hearty. This cooking method uses less oil than sautéing because the batter steams the vegetable while searing the outside.

Ingredients:

Serves 2-4

2 cups onions, carrots, broccoli, & mushrooms,
1/2 cup unbleached white flour
1/2 cup cornmeal flour
1 cup beer, sparkling or tonic water
safflower oil
soy sauce
sea salt
paper towels

Tempura Batter Method:

1. Combine flours & salt together. Gradually add liquid until you achieve a pancake batter consistency. If batter is too thick, gradually add liquid; if too thin, add flour.
2. Refrigerate 20-30 minutes prior to using.

Deep Fry Method:

1. Heat 5 inches of oil in a Dutch oven to 350°.
2. To test if oil is hot enough, drop a bit of batter into oil. If it sinks and pops right up, it is ready.
3. Dip vegetables in tempura batter and fry until golden brown.
4. Place on paper towel to absorb excess oil.
5. Sprinkle with either a few drops of soy sauce or sea salt unless you are serving a dipping sauce (see recipe on page 24).

Sassy Salsa

I was having company over for dinner and I needed a salsa. There were peaches and tomatoes and the rest is delicious history!

Ingredients:

Serves 2-4

2 cups tomatoes, diced
1 cup peach, peeled & diced
1/2 cup red onion, diced
1/4 cup cilantro, finely chopped
1/4 tsp. sea salt
1-2 tsps. extra virgin olive oil

Peeling Peaches Method:

1. Drop peaches into large pot of boiling water for 1-2 minutes. Remove and quickly rinse under cold water. Skins should peel right off.

Salsa Method:

1. In a large bowl, gently combine tomatoes, red onion, peaches, olive oil, cilantro and sea salt.

2. Let salsa sit at room temperature 1/2 hour prior to serving.

Game Day Bean Dip

It is possible to still eat healthy during a football game. This dip teams up well with the homemade tortilla chips.

Ingredients:

Serves 4-6

1 15oz. can refried black or pinto beans
1/2-1 cup salsa
1 cup guacamole
1/4 cup kalamata or black olives, diced
1/2-1 cup romaine lettuce, finely sliced
1/4 cup red onion, diced
1/4 cup cilantro, finely sliced
1/2 tsp. soy sauce

Method:

1. Put beans in skillet along with soy sauce. Stir and heat throughly.
2. Layer beans in a flat bowl.
3. Then layer guacamole, salsa, romaine, olives, red onions and cilantro.

You can add frozen or fresh corn to beans.

Homemade Tortilla Chips

Why spend money on tortilla chips when you can make your own.

Ingredients:

Serves 8-10

1 package corn tortillas
sea salt
safflower oil or any other oil for deep frying
paper towels

Method:

1. Cut corn tortillas into 8 sections.
2. Put 5 inches of oil into a Dutch oven and heat to 350º.
3. When oil is hot, put a few tortilla pieces into hot oil at a time without crowding the pan.
4. Use a metal spatula to dunk and turn chip so they cook evenly. Fry until golden brown.
5. Remove chips and drain on paper towel. Sprinkle with sea salt while still hot.

Seitan "Steak" Fingers

The texture and flavor of this "bar food" favorite will fool and satisfy the meat lovers at your table.

Ingredients:

Serves 2-4

1 package cooked seitan, left in chunks
1/2 cup unbleached white flour
1/2 cup whole-wheat pastry flour
1 cup beer, sparkling or tonic water
safflower oil
sea salt
paper towels

Northwestern Fry Sauce:

Only in the Northwest do they serve a fry sauce with French fries. This is also delicious with these seitan "steak" fingers.

1/2 cup of Vegenaise®
2 Tbsps. fruit-sweetened ketchup

Mix together & refrigerate 20 minutes prior to serving.

Method:

1. Whisk together flours, 1/2 tsp. salt, gradually adding liquid until you have a pancake batter consistency. If batter is too thick, add liquid. If too thin, add flour.

2. Refrigerate 20-30 minutes prior to using.

3. Heat 5 inches of oil in Dutch oven to 350°. To test if oil is ready, put a drop of batter into oil. If it sinks down and pops right up, it is ready.

4. Dip seitan in batter, fry until golden brown on each side. Place on paper towels to absorb excess oil.

5. Sprinkle with sea salt while still hot.

Soups

Butternut Squash Ginger Soup

Nothing says fall like a delicious squash soup. Sometimes a squash is so sweet, it tastes like candy!

Ingredients:

Serves 4

4 cups butternut squash, peeled & cubed
1 cup onion, diced
2-3 cups, water
sea salt
1 Tbsp. ginger juice, freshly grated
pumpkin seeds, roasted

Method:

1 Place squash and onion in an uncovered soup pot, add enough water to cover vegetables, add pinch sea salt and bring to boil.

2 Cover, simmer 20-25 minutes or until squash is fork tender.

3 Blend with either a hand-held immersion or regular blender, return to soup pot, add 1 tsp. sea salt and simmer 5-7 minutes. If soup is too thick, add more water along with more salt.

4 Grate ginger and with fingers squeeze ginger juice into soup.

5 Garnish with roasted pumpkin seeds.

Roasted Pumpkin Seeds Method:

Rinse pumpkin seeds and add to a dry skillet. On medium heat, stir continuously until golden brown and start to make a slight popping sound.

Carrot Soup
with Dill, Curry & Ginger

I describe this soup as a "bowl of warmth"! The curry and ginger combine nicely with the carrots and dill. It is simply delicious.

Ingredients:

Serves 2-4

4 cups carrots, peeled & diced
1 cup onion, diced
1/2 tsp. dried dill
1/2 tsp. curry powder or tumeric
1 Tbsp. olive oil
1 tsp. ginger juice, freshly squeezed
2-4 cups water

Method:

1. Heat oil in soup pot, sauté onions with a pinch of sea salt. Add dill and curry powder so the flavors bloom, sauté 1-2 minutes. Add carrots, sauté 1-2 minutes.

2. Cover carrots with water, approximately 2-3 cups. Cover, bring to boil, then reduce to a simmer for 20 minutes or until carrots are fork tender.

3. Blend soup, then add 1/2 tsp. sea salt, simmer 5 minutes. Taste to see if additional seasoning is needed.

4. Grate ginger and with fingers squeeze ginger juice into soup.

Corn Chowder

I love corn chowder, but not all the butter and cream. This new and improved chowder tastes so much like the real thing that when I served it, people swore it contained butter.

Ingredients:

Serves 4

1 medium onion diced
3 stalks celery, diced
1 large sweet potato, peeled & diced
4 cups corn, (5 large ears), cut off cobs (save cobs)
1 tsp. dried thyme or 2 tsps. fresh thyme, finely chopped
4 cups water or vegetable broth or 2 cups of each
sea salt
black pepper
2 Tbsps. olive oil
cilantro, chopped for garnish

Method:

1. In a heavy soup pot, heat oil, onions and a pinch of sea salt, sauté 1-2 minutes. Add thyme and 1/2 of the cut corn.
2. Add 2 cups water or broth. Using the back of your knife, scape the "corn milk" off the cut cobs and into the pot.
3. Bring to boil, cover and simmer 15 minutes. Use either a hand-held or regular blender to puree the chowder.
4. After pureed, add 1/2-1 tsp. sea salt, 1/4 tsp. black pepper, depending on taste, along with the sweet potato, celery and remainder of corn.
5. If soup is too thick, gradually add remaining liquid to desired consistency along with additional seasoning.
6. Cover, simmer 15-20 minutes or until potatoes are fork tender.
7. Garnish with fresh cilantro.

Mock "Chicken" Noodle Soup

This soup was inspired by a cooking class I took. We made a garbanzo bean soup, which smelled and tasted like chicken to me. So I thought, why not take that soup to the next level. This recipe will fool the best of them.

Ingredients:

Serves 2-4

2 15oz. cans of garbanzo beans, drained & rinsed
1 cup onion, diced
1 cup celery, diced
1 cup carrot, diced
1/2 cup small uncooked pasta (optional)
4 Tbsps. olive oil
4 cups water
1 tsp. black pepper
sea salt

Method:

1. Heat 3 Tbsps. oil in soup pot, sauté onion 1-2 minutes with pinch of sea salt. Add garbanzo beans and water. Cover, bring to a boil then simmer 5-10 minutes.

2. In separate skillet, heat remaining oil, sauté carrots with pinch of sea salt 1-2 minutes. Add celery and sauté 1-2 minutes.

3. Blend garbanzo bean mixture in a blender or with a hand-held immersion blender. Add 1/2 tsp. sea salt and simmer 5 minutes.

4. Add celery and carrots to garbanzo mixture along with uncooked pasta, 1/2 tsp. sea salt and 1 tsp. black pepper. Simmer 8-10 minutes.

5. If soup is too thick, gradually add water to achieve desired consistency along with more salt and pepper to achieve personal taste.

Pasta & White Bean Soup
with Kale

My husband just loves this soup. Served with a slice of pan-fried bread for dipping and he is in heaven!

Ingredients:

Serves 4

2 15oz. cans cannellini or great northern beans, drain & rinsed
1 cup onion, diced
1 cup kale, spine removed, bite-size pieces
1 tsp. dried rosemary
1/2 cup ditalini pasta or any small pasta
4 cups water
sea salt
black pepper
olive oil

Method:

1. Heat 1 Tbsp. oil in soup pot, add onion, pinch of sea salt and dried rosemary. Sauté until translucent. Add 1 can of beans and sauté 1-2 minutes. Add 2 cups water and bring to boil.
2. Cover, simmer 15 minutes.
3. Blend beans, add 1 tsp. sea salt and 1/2 tsp. black pepper. Add second can of beans, dry pasta and 1 cup water. Simmer 10 minutes or until pasta is soft.
4. If too thick, gradually add water to desired consistency along with additional seasoning.
5. Add kale when pasta is soft and simmer 1-2 minutes.

Split Pea Soup

What could be more comforting than split pea soup? It is one of my favorites because it is so rich and creamy. The cumin and chili powder give it a subtle kick.

Ingredients:

Serves 4

1 cup split peas, washed well (no need to soak)
1 cup onion, diced
1 cup carrot, quartered & diced 1/4" thick
4-5 cups water or vegetable broth
1 tsp. cumin (optional)
1/2 tsp. chili powder (optional)
sea salt
black pepper
olive or safflower oil
1 slice of bread, cubed for croutons

How to make croutons:

Heat skillet with 1/2 Tbsp. oil and add bread cubes. Stir continuously until golden brown.

Method:

1 Put split peas and 3 cups of water in an uncovered soup pot. Bring to a boil. With spoon, skim off the foam as it accumulates. Partially cover, reduce heat and simmer 50 minutes.

2 After 30 minutes, add 1 cup of water and continue to simmer. Be careful not to cove pot totally because foam will form and boi over.

3 After 50 minutes, blend soup, add onion, carrot, 1 tsp. sea salt, 1/4 tsp. black pepper, 1 tsp. cumin and 1/2 tsp. chili powder. Add 1/2 cup more water, simmer 30 minutes.

4 Taste and if needed, add 1 tsp. sea salt, le cook another 5 minutes.

Tomato Basil Soup

Tomato soup is the ultimate comfort food. Cannellini beans are a great way to make the soup creamy without the cream. They are also a wonderful source of protein and fiber.

Ingredients:

Serves 2-4

2 15oz. cans tomatoes, diced
1 15oz. can cannellini beans
1 Tbsp. tomato paste
1 cup onion, diced
3-4 cups water
1 Tbsp. olive oil
sea salt
black pepper
3/4 cup basil, finely sliced

Method:

1. Heat oil in soup pot, sauté onion with pinch of sea salt. Add tomato paste, sauté and blend into onions. Add cannellini beans, tomatoes and 3 cups of water. Stir.
2. Bring to a boil and simmer 15-20 minutes.
3. Blend with a hand-held immersion blender or in a regular blender, then season with 1 tsp. sea salt, 1/2 tsp. black pepper and add 1/2 cup basil. Simmer 5-7 minutes.
4. If soup is too thick, gradually add water and add more seasoning. Simmer 5-7 minutes.
5. Season to taste.
6. Garnish with basil.

"Where's the Beef?" Chili

Living in Idaho, beef rules. So, to win 2nd place out of 7 entries in a chili cook-off with this vegetarian chili was one of my proudest moments! You won't be asking, "Where's the beef?" with this recipe.

Ingredients:

Serves 4-6

2 15oz. cans of kidney, pinto or black beans, drained & rinsed
1 28oz. can crushed tomatoes
2 cups onion, diced
1 cup carrot, diced
2 cups corn, frozen
2 Tbsps. olive oil
2 Tbsps. tomato paste
2 Tbsps. chili powder
4 tsps. cumin
2 tsps. oregano
1/2 tsp. cinnamon
1/2 tsp. black pepper
sea salt
water
scallion or cilantro, finely sliced

Method:

1. Heat oil in large pot, sauté onions with several pinches of sea salt 1-2 minutes. Add carrots, sauté 1-2 minutes. Then tomato paste, 1 Tbsp. chili powder, 2 tsps. cumin, 1 tsp. oregano, 1 tsp. sea salt, 1/2 tsp. black pepper and sauté 1-2 minutes.

2. Add tomatoes (with the liquid) plus 1/2 can of water and stir well. Add additional water if you like a thinner consistency.

3. Cover, bring to boil, lower heat and simmer 15 -20 minutes. Add beans, 1 tsp. sea salt, remainder of chili powder, cumin, cinnamon, oregano, corn and simmer 10 minutes.

4. Taste and add more seasoning if needed. Simmer 5 minutes.

5. Garnish with scallion, cilantro or any other chili toppings you prefer.

This can be served over pasta.

White Bean, Mushroom Soup

This soup is so simple, yet filled with flavor. If you don't like rosemary, substitute it with another herb. Remember… the world is your oyster!

Ingredients:

Serves 2

1 cup mushrooms, sliced
1/2 cup onion, diced
1 15oz. can cannellini or great northern beans, drained & rinsed
1 Tbsp. olive oil
sea salt
1/2 tsp. dried rosemary
1/2 tsp. soy sauce
1/4 tsp. black pepper
1 1/2 cups water or vegetable broth

Method:

1. Heat oil in soup pot, add mushrooms and sauté until golden brown on both sides. Add onions, pinch of sea salt, soy sauce and sauté 1-2 minutes.

2. Add rosemary, beans, 1/2 tsp. sea salt and black pepper. Sauté 1-2 minutes, add water or broth.

3. Bring to boil, cover and simmer 15-20 minutes. Blend this soup if you like or let mushrooms and beans remain whole.

4. Taste and add more seasoning if needed. Simmer 5 minutes.

Sandwiches

Black Bean Burger

Seitan “Steak” Sandwich

Tempeh “Reuben” Sandwich

Tofu “Egg” Salad Sandwich

Tofu Marinara Sub

"D" LT&A

Black Bean Burgers

I have eaten my share of veggie burgers and decided I needed to come up with a better recipe. It is difficult to bind ingredients without eggs, but the mashed beans and couscous do quite well together.

Ingredients:

Serves 6-8

2 15oz. cans black beans, rinsed & dried
1 cup couscous
1/2 cup onion, diced
1/2 cup cilantro or basil, finely sliced
2 tsps. cumin
1-2 Tbsps. soy sauce
1 1/2 cup water
sea salt
safflower oil

These burgers need to be fried in a skillet or on a flat top - not directly on a grill.

Method:

1. Bring water to just under a boil, add couscous and pinch of sea salt. Stir, cover and take off heat 5-7 minutes.

2. In a large bowl, partially mash beans with a paper towel or potato masher.

3. Take a fork and fluff couscous into bean mixture. Add onion, cumin, cilantro and soy sauce. Stir with fork until well blended.

4. Wet hands to form 1/2 inch thick patties. Refrigerate 15-20 minutes prior to frying.

5. Heat 2 Tbsps. oil in frying pan, sauté patties 4 minutes on one side or until crisp and lightly browned. Add one drop of soy sauce prior to flipping patty and fry until golden brown. Only flip once.

6. Eat with a bun and all the fixings.

Seitan "Steak" Sandwich

This is one of my husband's favorite sandwiches. The combination of the soy sauce and seitan gives it a meaty flavor. Honestly, when I bring this sandwich to work, people often think I am eating meat!

Ingredients:

Serves 3

1 package cooked seitan, cut into thin slices
1/2 medium red onion, sliced into thin rings
1/2 tsp. soy sauce
light sesame or safflower oil
6 lettuce leaves
tomato, sliced thinly
Vegenaise® or mustard
6 slices sourdough or whole-wheat bread

Method:

1. Heat oil in skillet, saute seitan until lightly brown 1-2 minutes, sprinkle with soy sauce and flip seitan to sauté other side.
2. Spread Vegenaise® or mustard on bread, then layer onion, seitan, tomatoes and lettuce.
3. Top with other slice of bread already smeared with Vegenaise® or mustard.

Tempeh "Reuben" Sandwich

A good Reuben is one of life's little pleasures. It was my favorite sandwich growing up, so making over this sandwich was a must for me.

Ingredients:

Serves 2

1 block tempeh
2 Tbsps. sauerkraut
4 slices rye bread or preferred bread
soy sauce
safflower oil

Dressing Ingredients:

1/3 cup Vegenaise®
2 Tbsps. fruit-sweetened ketchup
1 tsp. sweet pickle relish (optional)

Tempeh Method:

1. Slice tempeh lengthwise, then with cut-side up, slice in half.
2. Heat 1 Tbsp. oil in skillet, sauté tempeh until golden brown on one side. Add one drop of soy sauce prior to flipping tempeh, sauté other side.
3. Add enough water to barely cover tempeh. Cover and simmer 20 minutes. When water is gone, remove and let cool.
4. Brush both sides of bread with oil and grill.
5. Spread generous amount of dressing on grilled bread, layer tempeh and sauerkraut on top.

Dressing Method:

Combine Vegenaise®, ketchup and relish and mix well. Chill 15 minutes prior to use.

Tofu "Egg" Salad Sandwich

I served tofu "egg" salad sandwiches at my wedding reception and no one had a clue it wasn't egg salad! Add whatever ingredients you normally use in egg salad and try this for your next lunch.

Ingredients:

Serves 6

1 16oz. block tofu, extra firm, cut into cubes
3/4 cup celery, diced small
1/2 cup red onion, finely diced
1/4 cup raisins, rinsed (optional)
water
sea salt
12 slices of bread, 6 rolls or wraps

Dressing Ingredients:

1/2 cup Vegenaise®
1/2 tsp. curry powder or turmeric
1/4 tsp. sea salt
1/8 tsp. black pepper
1/2 tsp. brown rice or apple cider vinegar
1 tsp. stone ground mustard

Method:

1. Combine all dressing ingredients together in a large bowl.
2. Bring water to a boil in a large saucepan, add one pinch of sea salt and add tofu cubes. Blanch 3 minutes.
3. Drain tofu, let cool on a plate. When cool, mash with a fork and put into large bowl.
4. Add celery, red onion, raisins and gently stir dressing into tofu mixture.
5. Cover and chill 2-24 hours.
6. Serve on favorite bread with lettuce.

Tofu Marinara Sub

Preparing tofu this way always reminds me of eggplant parmigiana. The outside is crispy, and tastes SO good with the marinara sauce. This is definitely not rabbit food!

Ingredients:

Serves 4

1 16oz. block tofu, extra firm, cut lengthwise into 4 one-inch thick slices
1 cup unbleached all-purpose flour
1 cup Italian bread crumbs
1 cup soy, almond or rice milk
1-2 Tbsps. olive oil
1 cup marinara sauce
4 romaine lettuce leaves
4 whole-wheat submarine rolls

This tofu can also be served on its own with just marinara sauce and a side of pasta.

Method:

1 Press excess water out of tofu slices by covering them with either a paper towel or cotton cloth and literally pressing it ou using your hands. You could also place a cookie sheet with a weight on top of tofu

2 Set-up 3 dredging stations with flat-bottom bowls. Fill one with flour, one with soy milk, and one with Italian breadcrumbs.

3 Take pressed tofu and coat it with flour (shaking off any excess), then coat with soy milk and then bread crumbs.

4 Heat oil in cast-iron skillet and sauté unti golden brown on each side. Place tofu on paper towel to absorb excess oil.

5 Gently heat marinara sauce in saucepan. Assemble sandwiches.

"D"LT & A

Dulse, Lettuce, Tomato & Avocado

The BLT is a classic comfort food sandwich. The fried dulse is the perfect substitute for the bacon. I love to shop at the farmer's market and come home with a great tomato and lettuce and make this sandwich.

Ingredients:

Serves 4

fried dulse (see page 96 for recipe)
4 romaine lettuce leaves
4 tomato slices
1 avocado, sliced
Vegenaise®
8 slices sourdough or whole-wheat bread

Method:

1. Toast, grill or fry bread.

2. Spread Vegenaise® on bread, layer lettuce, tomato, avocado and dulse.

Main Courses

Beans on Polenta

This is my go-to meal when I want something warm and comforting. Often times, I serve the beans on soft polenta instead of letting it harden in a baking dish and pan frying it.

Beans Ingredients:

Serves 4

2 15oz. cans pinto beans, rinsed & drained
1 cup onions, diced
1 tsp. cumin
sea salt
olive oil
1/2 cup water
scallions, sliced for garnish

Polenta Ingredients:

1 cup instant cornmeal
4 cups water
1/2 cup corn, fresh or frozen
1 pinch sea salt
soy sauce
olive oil

Beans can also be served on pan-fried bread.

Beans Method:

1. Heat 1 Tbsp. oil in a cast iron skillet, sauté onions with a pinch of sea salt 1-2 minutes. Add beans.
2. Stir in 1 tsp. sea salt, cumin and water, cover and sauté 15-20 minutes. Stir occasionally until mixture gets nice and creamy. Add more water if needed.
3. Garnish with scallion.

Polenta Method:

1. Bring water to a boil in a large saucepan and gradually add the cornmeal and 1 pinch of sea salt while whisking at the same time. Let it come to a boil, reduce heat, and cover.
2. Stir often until thick and creamy, approximately 20 minutes.
3. When it is almost done, add corn and stir until it is well blended. Pour into an 8x8 baking dish. Let cool. Slice into squares.
4. Heat 1 Tbsp. oil in skillet and sauté polenta. Prior to flipping, pour one drop of soy sauce and sauté until lightly golden.

Lasagna
with Spinach, Mushroom & Onion

Who doesn't like lasagna. The problem is it's usually loaded with cheese. I found when I blended the tofu, it actually had the appearance and taste of ricotta cheese.

Ingredients:

Serves 10-12

1 16oz. block tofu, extra-firm
1/4 cup sun-dried tomatoes, oil packed
1/2 cup kalamata olives, pitted
3/4 cup, fresh basil
2 10oz. boxes frozen chopped spinach, defrosted
5 cups mushrooms, sliced
4 cups onions, finely sliced half moons
sea salt
black pepper
5 cups marinara sauce
12 sheets lasagna noodles
olive oil

Lasagna Noodle Method:

1 Place uncooked lasagna noodles in a large baking dish, cover with boiling water for 20 minutes. Then use.

Spinach Method:

2 Place a cotton kitchen towel in a bowl, empty spinach into towel, wrap tightly and squeeze out excess liquid.

Tofu Mixture Method:

3 In food processor, blend tofu, sun-dried tomatoes, olives, 1/2 cup basil, 1 tsp. sea salt and 1/2 tsp. black pepper. Add 1 tsp. olive oil. Pulse until well blended and has paste-like consistency.

Filling Mixture Method:

1 Heat oil in large skillet, sauté onions, mushrooms and spinach separately with large pinches of salt and pepper. When spinach is almost done, add cooked onions and mushrooms and sauté together 1-2 minutes to combine together.

2 Place in bowl and let cool prior to building lasagna.

(continued >>)

Lasagna
with Spinach, Mushroom & Onion

(<< continued)

Build Lasagna Method:

1. Preheat oven to 350°.

2. Spread 1 cup marinara sauce on bottom of a 9 x 13 baking dish.

3. Place 3 pasta sheets on top of sauce. Spread 1/3 tofu mixture on pasta, spread 1/3 spinach mixture on top of tofu. Spread 1 cup marinara sauce on top of spinach mixture. Repeat sequence two more times.

4. Top with last 3 pasta sheets and 1 cup marinara sauce.

5. Cover with foil, bake 45-50 minutes.

6. Garnish with fresh basil, let stand 15 minutes prior to serving.

Lentil Bolognese

This is one warming, filling and just plain delicious pasta dish. The lentils makes this dish so hearty, it will definitely fill you up!

Ingredients:

Serves 4-6

1 cup green or red lentils
3 cups marinara sauce
8oz. whole-wheat rigatoni
1/2 cup onions, diced
1/2 cup carrots, diced
1/2 cup celery, diced
olive oil
sea salt
black pepper
1 Tbsp. tomato paste
1 tsp. dried oregano
basil for garnish, finely sliced

Method:

1. Place lentils on a plate and sort through them for debris or damaged lentils. Rinse and put in saucepan, cover with water by 2 inches.

2. Bring to boil, reduce heat and simmer 20-25 minutes. When they are 80% done (squeeze one and feel), add 1/2 tsp. sea salt. If they are soaking up the water and are not done, add more water and continue to cook until soft.

3. In a separate large Dutch oven, heat 3 Tbsps. olive oil, sauté onions with pinch of sea salt 1-2 minutes, add carrots, sauté 1-2 minutes, add celery, sauté 1-2 minutes, then add tomato paste and combine well.

4. When lentils are soft, add to sautéed veggies along with the pasta sauce, 1 tsp. sea salt, oregano and 1/2 tsp. black pepper. Cover, simmer 15-20 minutes, stirring occasionally.

5. Fill large pot with water, bring to boil, add 1 Tbsp. sea salt and pasta. Cook al dente. When pasta is ready, add to lentil sauce and mix together. Add a 1/4 cup of the salted pasta water, stir until sauce is combined well and coating pasta.

6. Garnish with basil.

Mexican Bean Cups

For 6 years, I taught healthy cooking classes to 5th, 6th & 7th graders. I was thinking what would be a yummy lunch they could pick up and eat with their hands. Mexican Bean Cups were born and the kids loved them!

Ingredients:

Serves 8

8 egg roll wrappers
1 15oz. can black beans, drained & rinsed
2/3 cup salsa
1/2 cup red onion, diced
1/2 cup corn, fresh or frozen
1/4-1/2 cup safflower oil
scallion or cilantro, finely sliced for garnish

You can add additional toppings such as guacamole or shredded lettuce.

Method:

1. Preheat oven to 350°.
2. Grease one cupcake or muffin tin with oil. Press wrappers into tins. If they overlap too much, cut excess off with scissors.
3. Brush wrappers with oil and bake 5-8 minutes or until golden brown. Remove from tin and let cool.
4. Blanch (see pg. 116 for blanching method) beans 1-2 minutes and then corn for 30-45 seconds. In a bowl, combine beans, corn, onion and salsa.
5. Take approximately 2 Tbsps. bean mixture and place in each wrapper.
6. Garnish with scallion or cilantro.

Pasta Marinara
with Kalamata Olives, Capers & Basil

The olives and capers turn an ordinary plate of pasta into something quite extraordinary! You can use your favorite jarred marinara sauce for this recipe and no one will know the difference.

Ingredients:

Serves 4

8oz. of any pasta preferred
1 cup onion, diced
2 cups tomatoes, crushed
1 cup kalamata olives, pitted & halved
1/2 cup sun-dried tomatoes, oil packed diced
1 Tbsp. capers
1 Tbsp. tomato paste
2 Tbsps. olive oil
1 garlic clove, peeled & minced (optional)
1 tsp. dried oregano
sea salt
1/4 cup basil, finely sliced for garnish
1/2 cup pasta cooking water
water

Pasta Method:

1 Follow pasta cooking instructions but cook al dente. Reserve 1/2 cup pasta cooking water.

Sauce Method:

1 Heat oil in large sauté pan, add onion with pinch of sea salt, sauté 1-2 minutes. Add garlic, saute 1-2 minutes, then tomato paste and sauté 1-2 minutes.

2 Add tomatoes, 1/2 tsp. salt, oregano, cover and simmer 10-15 minutes. Add olives, capers and sun-dried tomatoes, stir into sauce. Let simmer until pasta is done.

Preparation of Dish:

1 Add pasta to sauce along with 1/4-1/2 cups reserved pasta water. Simmer while combining it together until sauce thickens and water is absorbed (tongs work well for this).

2 Garnish with basil.

Shepherd's Pie

While living in Boston, I developed a love for Shepherd's Pie. It is a classic comfort food dish and traditionally is made with lamb. I substituted black beans for the lamb and added veggies. This dish is still hearty and perfect on a cold, winter's night.

Ingredients:

Serves 2-4

1 cup onion, diced
1 cup carrot, diced
1 cup peas, fresh or frozen
1 cup corn, fresh or frozen
1 15oz. can black beans, drained & rinsed
1 1/2 Tbsps. tomato paste
3 Tbsps. soy sauce
3 Tbsps. sesame or olive oil
1-2 lbs. white potatoes, (approx. 2 lg. potatoes), washed & diced
sea salt
black pepper
1/4 cup water

Method:

1. Preheat oven to 400°.
2. Heat oil in large skillet, sauté onion with pinch of sea salt 1-2 minutes, add carrots and sauté 2-3 minutes. Add tomato paste in hot spot of skillet and let sauté 1 minute, then add soy sauce and blend together well.
3. Add beans, peas, corn and 1/4 cup water and mix together.
4. Put bean mixture into an 8 x 8 baking dish and level with offset spatula.

Mashed Potatoes Method:

1. In a large pot, cover potatoes with cold water, add 1-2 Tbsps. salt, bring to boil. Simmer 15-20 minutes until potatoes are fork tender. Drain potatoes, but reserve cooking water.
2. Return potatoes to hot pot and start to mash. Gradually add cooking water so potatoes have a smooth consistency. Add 1/4-1/2 tsp. sea salt and 1/4 tsp. black pepper or more to personal taste. Drizzle with olive oil and mix together.

Putting Dish Together:

Spread mashed potatoes on top of bean mixture and smooth out. Bake 20-25 minutes. Let stand 5-10 minutes before serving.

Stuffed Squash
with Sourdough & Seitan Dressing

Many people worry about what to serve vegetarians when they come for Thanksgiving or actually any dinner. This squash dish is so delicious everyone will want it.

Ingredients:

Serves 4-6

1 large buttercup, kabocha squash or hokkaido pumpkin
4 cups sourdough or whole wheat bread, cubed
1/2 cup onion, diced
1/2 cup seitan, cubed (optional)
4 to 5 mushrooms, diced
1/4 cup celery, diced
1/2 cup water
1 tsp. dried sage
soy sauce
sesame oil (toasted or light)
sea salt

Method:

1. Preheat oven to 450°.
2. Cut top of squash out like a Jack-O-Lantern and clean out seeds.
3. Heat 2 Tbsps. oil in large skillet, sauté onion with pinch of salt 1-2 minutes. Add mushrooms and sage, saute 2-3 minutes. Add seitan, 1 tsp. soy sauce then celery and sauté 3 minutes. Place in bowl.
4. Combine bread and water in large bowl along with 1-2 tsps. soy sauce and mix thoroughly. Gently stir in cooked seitan and vegetables.
5. Stuff hollowed-out squash with dressing and put top on. Wrap squash stem with aluminum foil to prevent burning.
6. Rub vegetable oil on squash skin, place in glass baking dish. Bake 30-35 minutes or until squash can be pierced with either a fork, bamboo skewer or chopstick.
7. If squash is not tender, continue to cook. You can remove the top and cook until done.

Sushi
with Avocado, Carrot & Cucumber

This is a wonderful way to use leftover rice. Homemade sushi can be eaten as a snack or quick meal. Experiment with different combinations.

Ingredients:

Serves 1 roll per person

1 cup leftover brown or white rice per one sushi roll
1 toasted nori seaweed sheet
1 bamboo mat
3-4 pieces of cucumber, sliced finely lengthwise
3-4 pieces of carrot, sliced finely & blanched
1 tsp. stone ground mustard

Method:

1. Place one sheet of nori, shiny side down, on bamboo sushi mat, with shortest side closest to you and to the edge of the mat
2. Wet hands slightly and press rice down with fingers. Cover 3/4 of nori sheet, leaving 2 inches open at the top.
3. Spread mustard on edge of rice and then place fillings on top. Don't overload the bottom edge with too many vegetables, it will make it difficult to roll.
4. Roll sushi mat with nori up to the 2 inch gap. Wet the exposed nori with your fingers, then roll the nori closed.
5. Let it set a few minutes before cutting the nori roll into eight pieces.

Cutting Nori Roll Method:

Wet knife, cut nori roll in half. Wet knife again, cut each half in half, then repeat with the remaining halves until you have 8 pieces.

Vegetable Fried Rice

This is such a quick dish to make and a great solution for what to do with leftover veggies. You can always add beans to make this a main course.

Ingredients:

Serves 4

2 cups leftover brown or white rice
1/2 cup onions, diced
1/2 cup carrots, diced
1/2 cup diced celery, peas, mushrooms or any combo vegetables
1 Tbsp. light sesame or olive oil
sea salt
soy sauce
1 Tbsp. ginger juice, freshly grated
1/4 cup scallions, finely sliced as a garnish

Method:

1 Heat oil in skillet. Add onions with pinch o sea salt, sauté 1-2 minutes. Add additiona vegetables separately, sauté 1-2 minutes before adding each veggie.

2 Place rice on top of sautéed vegetables, add approx. 1/4-1/2 cup water, cover and simmer 5-7 minutes.

3 Check to see if rice is getting soft. If it is, add 1/2 tsp. soy sauce, stir well.

4 Cover, sauté another 5 minutes until rice is sticky. Then add ginger juice, stir and garnish with scallions.

It is important not to use freshly made rice. Either make rice several hours earlier or use leftover rice.

Side Dishes

Brussel Sprouts

Many people do not consider brussel sprouts comfort food, but I do. They are one of my favorite sides at Thanksgiving. This dish turned my brother-in-law from a brussel sprout hater to lover!

Ingredients:

Serves 8

1 bag, brussel sprouts
olive oil
sea salt
soy sauce
4 lemon wedges

Method:

1. Cut off ends of sprouts, keep enough to hold sprout together. Remove old, outside leaves and cut in half.

2. Heat 2 Tbsps. oil in large skillet, put brussel sprouts cut-side down, sprinkle with large pinch of sea salt. When caramelized, sprinkle with 1/2 tsp. soy sauce, flip sprouts, sauté 3 4 minutes.

3. When both sides are caramelized, pour 1/4 cup water into skillet, cover and simmer 5-7 minutes. When sprouts are tender they are done.

4. Squeeze a little lemon juice on sprouts prior to serving.

Coleslaw

Coleslaw is a great side dish for many entrees and sandwiches. It should be light and refreshing, but often the mayonnaise weighs it down. Vegenaise® makes this recipe light, refreshing and simply delicious!

Ingredients:

Serves 4

1/2 head green cabbage, finely sliced
1/2 head red cabbage, finely sliced
4 celery stalks, diced
1 carrot, grated
1/2 red onion, sliced in half moons

Dressing Ingredients:

1 1/2 cups Vegenaise®
1 Tbsp. brown rice or apple cider vinegar
1 tsp. sea salt
1/2 tsp. black pepper

Method:

1. Combine vegetables in a large bowl.
2. In a separate bowl, combine the dressing ingredients. Add dressing to vegetables and toss together (tongs work best) until coated well.
3. Refrigerate 30 minutes prior to serving.

Down-Home Cornbread

There is nothing better than chili and cornbread. Often times it is so sweet it tastes more like dessert. This recipe is still sweet, but not overpowering and has the same texture and delicious corn flavor of traditional cornbread.

Ingredients:

Serves 8

2 cups cornmeal
1 cup unbleached all-purpose flour
3 tsps. baking powder
1/3 cup safflower or vegetable oil
5 Tbsps. maple syrup
2 cups soy milk
2 tsps. apple cider vinegar
1/2 tsp. sea salt

Method:

1. Preheat oven to 350°.
2. Line a 9 x13 baking pan with parchment paper.
3. Whisk soy milk and vinegar together, set aside.
4. Sift dry ingredients together (cornmeal, flour, baking powder and salt).
5. Whisk oil and syrup into the soy milk mixture until well blended (approximately 2 minutes).
6. Pour wet ingredients into dry ingredients, mix together well.
7. Pour batter into baking pan, bake 25-30 minutes. Insert a knife or toothpick into center of cornbread to test if done. If batter sticks to it, bake another 5 minutes.
8. Test again and if needed, bake another 5 minutes. Repeat until knife or toothpick comes out clean.

Fried Dulse

Frying this seaweed transforms it from soft and red to crispy and brown! It reminds me of bacon, so I use it as a side dish for tofu scramble and on sandwiches and salads.

Ingredients:

Serves 4-6

1 package Maine Coast dulse seaweed
soy sauce
1 Tbsp. safflower or sesame oil
paper towels

Method:

1. Separate dulse to sauté evenly.
2. Heat oil in cast iron skillet, add dulse.
3. Saute 1-3 minutes, sprinkle with 1/2 tsp. soy sauce, stir until brown and crispy.
4. Place on paper towels to soak up excess oil.

Kale Chips

Kale chips are a great substitute for commercial chips. These are so delicious and SO good for you!

Ingredients:

Serves 8

1 bunch kale, washed, stems removed
1 Tbsp. olive oil
1 tsp. sea salt
parchment paper

Method:

1. Preheat oven to 350°.
2. Make sure kale is thoroughly dry and cut into bite-size pieces.
3. Brush olive oil on both sides of kale or use your fingers to coat kale with oil.
4. Place on a cookie sheet lined with parchment paper.
5. Bake until edges are brown, not burnt (approximately 10-15 minutes).
6. Remove from oven, sprinkle with sea salt while they are still hot.

Mashed Potatoes
with Caramelized Onions

It's usually the butter and cream that makes mashed potatoes so yummy. I figured out a way to make potatoes creamy without the added saturated fat and cholesterol. The caramelized onions add a nice rich flavor to this dish.

Ingredients:

Serves 4

2 lbs. Yukon Gold potatoes, washed & diced (with or without skins)
1 cup onions, sliced into half moons
olive oil
sea salt
black pepper
chives, sliced finely for garnish

Add horseradish or roasted garlic to mashed potatoes for a different flavor.

Method:

1. Put potatoes in large pot, cover with cold water, add 1 Tbsp. sea salt, bring to boil. Simmer 15-20 minutes or until fork tender.
2. Drain potatoes in colander over large bowl to reserve cooking water.
3. Put potatoes back in hot pan, mash with potato masher and gradually add reserved cooking water to desired texture. Add a drizzle of olive oil, 1/2 tsp. sea salt and 1/4 tsp. black pepper.
4. Stir onions into potatoes. Taste, add additional seasoning if needed. Garnish with chives.

Caramelized Onion Method:

1. In a large skillet, heat 2-3 Tbsps. olive oil, add onions with pinch of sea salt. Sauté 2-3 minutes.
2. Lower flame and sauté slowly until golden brown, stirring occasionally, approximately 20 minutes.

Polenta Fries

I am not sure how I thought of these, but I am certainly glad I did! They are crunchy on the outside and still a bit soft on the inside. Dipped in your favorite marinara sauce, these can be an appetizer or side dish.

Ingredients:

Serves 2

1 18oz. pre-made polenta roll
olive oil
sea salt
1 cup marinara sauce

Method:

1. Preheat oven to 350°.
2. Cut 8 inch polenta roll into 4 inch halves. Cut halves lengthwise and then cut into 1/2 inch slices.
3. Brush polenta slices with olive oil, sprinkle with sea salt. Layer on cookie sheet.
4. Bake 15 minutes on one side, turn when they are a bit crispy. Bake additional 10-15 minutes.
5. Gently warm marinara sauce for dipping.

Homemade polenta would work too. Just let polenta harden in a baking dish and cut into 1/2 inch slices.

Rutabaga & Onion Hash

This recipe came about because I had some rutabagas and needed to bring a side dish to a friend's brunch. Everyone loved it!

Ingredients:

Serves 4

2 lbs. rutabagas (approx. 2 large), peeled & diced
1 onion, diced
sea salt
1/8 tsp. black pepper
safflower oil
1/4 cup chives, sliced for garnish

Method:

1. Heat 1-2 Tbsp. oil in cast iron skillet. Layer rutabaga in skillet, sprinkle with large pinch of sea salt and let caramelize (approx. 5 minutes). When lightly brown, turn and sauté other side.

2. Stir in onions along with another pinch of sea salt and black pepper, sauté 1-2 minutes.

3. Cover, lower heat and let sauté 5-7 minutes or until fork tender. Stirring occasionally.

4. Taste, add more seasoning if preferred.

5. Garnish with chives.

Sweet Potato & Parsnip Fries

Sweet potatoes and parsnips are great alternatives for fries. They are a good source of beta carotene and do not raise your blood sugar as quickly as white potatoes.

Ingredients:

Serves 4-6

1 sweet potato or yam
1 parsnip
sea salt
olive oil
paper towels

Method:

1 Preheat oven to 400°.

2 Peel and slice vegetables into 1/2 inch strips. Coat vegetables with oil and sea salt and layer on cookie sheet. Make sure they are not crowded.

3 Bake 10-15 minutes until lightly brown, flip veggies and bake other side.

4 Drain on paper towels.

5 Sprinkle with sea salt while still hot.

Sweet Yams
with Apples & Apricots

I used to love the traditional marshmallow and sweet potato dish. So I improved it. Instead of marshmallows, why not maple-coated pecans! Meet my new favorite Thanksgiving sweet potato dish.

Ingredients:

Serves 4-6

2 lbs. garnet yams, peeled & sliced into 1/4 inch slices
2 Granny Smith apples, peeled & cored and thinly sliced
20 dried apricots, rinsed
1 cup apple juice, not concentrate
maple syrup (optional)
sea salt
safflower oil
1 cup pecans, toasted & roughly chopped

Method:

1. Preheat oven to 375°. Lightly coat 8 x 8 baking dish with oil.
2. Pour maple syrup in small bowl, and with pastry brush, lightly brush maple syrup on top-side of each yam slice.
3. Cover bottom of baking dish with one layer of yams, arranging slices in 4 overlapping rows, like roof tiles. Sprinkle a pinch of sea salt over yams.
4. Cover yams with apple slices, then apricots. Cover apricots with another layer of maple-syrup coated yams. Sprinkle with sea salt.
5. Pour apple juice gently down side of baking dish. Cover with foil, bake 40 minutes.
6. In small bowl, coat pecans with maple syrup. After 40 minutes, uncover yams and spread nuts on top. Bake 15 minutes uncovered.
7. Let stand 10 minutes before serving.

Salads

Asian Noodle Salad
with Peanut Dressing

This salad has such a yummy richness to it. It's great as a main course or a side dish. Kids love it! You can substitute pasta or somen noodles for the udon.

Salad Ingredients:

Serves 4-6

1 8oz. package udon noodles
1 1/2 cups edamame, shelled
1 cup carrots, matchsticks
1/2 cup red pepper, sliced
1/2 cup cilantro, sliced for garnish
2 Tbsps. sesame seeds, toasted

Peanut Dressing Ingredients:

1 large garlic clove, peeled & crushed
1/2 cup smooth peanut or almond butter
1/2 cup cilantro, rinsed
1/4 soy sauce
1/4 cup rice wine vinegar
3 Tbsps. toasted sesame oil
1/3 cup warm water
1/4 tsp. sea salt
2 tsps. ginger juice, freshly grated

Salad Method:

1. Cook udon noodles according to package instructions. If using udon noodles, rinse 3 times in cold water.

2. Bring large pot of water to boil, add sea salt and blanch edamame 30-60 seconds or until they float. Then carrots. Remove, drain well, cool on a plate.

3. When vegetables are cool, add to noodles along with the red pepper. Slowly pour dressing to desired amount. Use tongs to coat noodles with dressing.

4. Chill 1/2 hour prior to serving. Garnish with cilantro and sesame seeds.

Dressing Method:

Put all ingredients into blender and blend until smooth.

Toast Sesame Seed Method:

Rinse sesame seeds, put in skillet. Heat pan and stir continuously until golden brown.

Brown Basmati Rice Salad
with Garbanzo Beans, Raisins & Balsamic Dressing

For this salad, you can use leftover rice or make it fresh. The sweetness of the raisins combined with the garbanzo beans is absolutely delicious!

Ingredients:

Serves 4

1 cup brown basmati rice, rinsed
1 1/2 cups water
sea salt
1/2 cup golden raisins, rinsed
1/2 cup red onion, diced
1 15oz. can garbanzo beans
1 cup English cucumber, diced
1/4 cup pine nuts, toasted

Ingredients for Dressing:

1/2 tsp. oregano
1/2 tsp. thyme
1 tsp. stone ground mustard
1/2 tsp. sea salt
1/3 cup balsamic vinegar
2/3 cup olive oil

Rice Method:

1. In saucepan, add rice, water and pinch of salt. Bring to boil, cover and simmer 35 minutes. When done, let stand 10 minutes. Fluff rice into bowl to cool.

2. In another saucepan, bring water to boil. Add pinch of sea salt, blanch beans 2-3 minutes. Remove from water, drain, let cool on a plate.

3. When cool, add beans, veggies, raisins to rice and gently stir in dressing.

4. Garnish with pine nuts.

Dressing Method:

Whisk all ingredients together in a small bowl, except oil. Then slowly whisk in oil until dressing is creamy.

Pine Nuts Method:

Heat a dry skillet over medium heat. Add pine nuts and stir continuously until golden brown. Transfer to bowl to cool.

Crunchy Blanched Salad
with Cabbage, Celery & Carrots

When the summer ends, I stop eating lettuce and often make blanched vegetable salad. It is crispy, colorful and crunchy! A combination of root, round and leafy green vegetables work best. It is best served at room temperature.

Ingredients:

Serves 3

1 cup purple cabbage, diced
1 cup carrot, diced
1 cup celery, diced
sea salt

Blanching Method:

1. Fill pot with water, bring to boil (uncovered) and add pinch of sea salt.
2. Blanch each vegetable separately, in the order from mildest to strongest tasting or lightest to darkest in color.
3. Place vegetable in boiling water (water stops boiling when vegetable is added). Boil uncovered until color is brightest (approx. 30-60 seconds depending on size of vegetable).
4. Remove vegetables from boiling water, place on plate and drain well. Let cool before combining vegetables.
5. Serve blanched salad plain, with a dressing or a splash of brown rice vinegar or lemon juice.

Greek Couscous Salad
with Lemon-Oregano Dressing

This is my "go to" salad when I need to bring a dish to a potluck or picnic and NO ONE is disappointed! You can always substitute pasta or quinoa for the couscous.

Ingredients:

Serves 4-6

1 1/2 cup water
1 cup couscous
sea salt
1 15oz. can garbanzo beans, blanched
1/2 cup grape tomatoes, halved
1/2 cup red onion, diced
1/2 cup cucumber, diced
1/2 avocado, diced
1/2 cup kalamata olives, pitted & halved
1/2 cup pine nuts, toasted

Dressing Ingredients:

2/3 cup olive oil
3 Tbsps. lemon juice, fresh
1/2 tsp. oregano
1/2 tsp. sea salt
1/4 tsp. black pepper

Couscous Method:

1. Heat water in covered saucepan until right under boiling point. Add couscous and pinch of salt.
2. Turn heat off and let stand 5-10 minutes. Use back of fork to fluff couscous into large bowl.
3. After couscous is cooled, add vegetables, olives and beans. Gently mix in dressing.
4. Garnish with toasted pine nuts.

Dressing Method:

1. Whisk sea salt, oregano, black pepper and lemon juice together in a bowl.
2. Then slowly whisk in olive oil until creamy in color.

Mediterranean Pasta Salad

I see the same ol' pasta salad at every picnic, so I decided to take it up a notch. You can use any shaped pasta and add any vegetables you choose.

Ingredients:

Serves 6-8

16oz. farfalle pasta
1 cucumber, peeled & diced
1 cup red onion, diced
1 container of grape tomatoes, halved
1/2 cup kalamata olives, pitted & halved
1/4 cup pine nuts, toasted
fresh basil, sliced finely for garnish

Dressing Ingredients:

2/3 cup of extra virgin olive oil
1/3 cup balsamic vinegar
1 clove of garlic, finely diced (optional)
2 tsps. dried oregano
1 tsp. sea salt
1/2 tsp. blk. pepper

Method:

1. Cook pasta al dente, rinse and cool before adding vegetables & dressing.
2. Whisk the balsamic vinegar, garlic, oregano, salt & pepper in a small bowl. Then slowly whisk in oil until dressing is creamy.
3. When pasta is cool, add vegetables and olives. Gently toss with dressing.
4. Garnish with pine nuts & basil.

Toast Pine Nuts:

Heat a dry skillet over medium heat, add pine nuts and stir continuously until golden brown. Transfer to small bowl to cool.

Mustard Dill Potato Salad

This is not your Grandmother's potato salad. Making potato salad with a vinaigrette instead of a mayonnaise or sour cream based dressing, not only lightens it dramatically, but won't spoil in the hot sun. This salad can be served chilled or at room temperature.

Ingredients:

Serves 4-6

2 lbs. red bliss potatoes, cut into chunks (not peeling is a preference)
1 cup celery, diced
1/2 cup scallion, finely sliced
1/4 cup fresh dill, chopped for garnish
sea salt

Dressing Ingredients:

1 Tbsp. apple cider or brown rice vinegar
6 Tbsps. olive oil
2 Tbsps. stone ground mustard
1 tsp. sea salt
1/2 tsp. dried dill
1/4 tsp. black pepper

Potato Method:

1. Place cut potatoes in a large pot, cover with cold water, add 1-2 Tbsps. sea salt, bring to a boil.
2. Reduce heat, simmer 15-20 minutes or until fork-tender. Drain and put in a large bowl.

Potato Salad Method:

1. Pour half of dressing onto the warm potatoes and gently mix.
2. Add celery, scallion and fresh dill. Stir gently. If you are serving potato salad chilled, add rest of dressing prior to serving. Otherwise, add rest of dressing after you add the vegetables and gently mix together.

Dressing Method:

Whisk all ingredients together, except olive oil. Then slowly whisk in oil until dressing is creamy.

Southwestern Cobb Salad

The Cobb Salad is the mother of all salads. Black beans are a healthy substitute for the traditional use of meat, cheese and bacon. A lime-cilantro vinaigrette keeps this salad ligh and refreshing.

Salad Ingredients:

Serves 4

8 cups romaine lettuce, cut into bite-size pieces
1 cup black beans, blanched
1 cup corn, (fresh or frozen) blanched
1 cup jicima, peeled & diced
1 cup red onion, diced
1 cup avocado, diced
4 corn tortillas, sliced in strips
sea salt
paper towels

Lime-Cilantro Dressing Ingredients:

1 cup cilantro
1 tsp. sea salt
1 tsp. oregano
1 tsp. cumin
1/3 cup lime juice, freshly squeezed (approx. 2 limes)
2/3 cup olive oil

Method:

1. Layer ingredients in sections on top of lettuce either on a plate on in a large bowl.

Dressing Method:

1. Combine first 5 ingredients in a blender and slowly pour oil in until blended.
2. Chill 20 minutes before dressing salad.

Tortilla Strips Method:

1. Heat 5 inches of oil in saucepan for deep frying. Drop a piece of tortilla in oil to see if it is hot enough. If it hits bottom and pops up quickly, oil is ready.
2. Fry tortilla strips until golden brown. Remove from oil, drain on paper towel to absorb excess oil.
3. Sprinkle with sea salt while still hot.

Tofu "Egg" Salad

This salad is delicious on a bed of lettuce, with crackers or stuffed in a tomato. Add whatever ingredients you normally use in your egg salad.

Ingredients:

Serves 6

1 16 oz. block tofu, extra firm, cut into cubes
3/4 cup celery, diced small
1/2 cup red onion, finely diced
1/4 cup raisins, rinsed (optional)
1/4 cup toasted, slivered almonds
water
sea salt

Dressing Ingredients:

1/2 cup Vegenaise®
1/2 tsp. curry powder or turmeric
1/4 tsp. sea salt
1/8 tsp. black pepper
1/2 tsp. brown rice or apple cider vinegar
1 tsp. stone ground mustard

Method:

1. Combine all dressing ingredients together in a large bowl.
2. Bring water to a boil in a large saucepan, add one pinch of sea salt and add tofu cubes. Blanch 3 minutes.
3. Drain tofu, let cool on a plate. When cool, mash with a fork and put in large bowl.
4. Add celery, red onion, raisins to tofu and gently stir dressing into mixture.
5. Cover and chill 2-24 hours.
6. Garnish with toasted slivered almonds right before serving.

Summer Salad
with Black Beans and Corn

The corn and black beans are a great combination. This refreshing summer salad can stand on its own as a main course.

Ingredients:

Serves 4

1 15oz. can black beans
1 head romaine lettuce, chopped
1 cup fresh corn, blanched or frozen corn, defrosted
1/2 cup red onion, diced
1/2 cup grape tomatoes, halved
1/2 cup kalamata olives, pitted & diced
1/2 cup pine nuts, toasted

Dressing Ingredients:

1/3 cup lemon juice, freshly squeezed
2/3 cup olive oil
1 tsp. sea salt
1 tsp. cumin
1 tsp. oregano

Method:

1 Heat pot of water to a boil, add a pinch of sea salt. Blanch fresh corn 30 seconds. Add black beans when water comes to a boil again, blanch 1 minute. Let cool before adding to salad.

2 In a large bowl, combine lettuce, corn, onion, tomatoes, olives and beans.

3 Gently toss salad with dressing.

4 Garnish with pine nuts.

Dressing Method:

Whisk together sea salt, cumin, oregano and lemon juice in a bowl. Slowly whisk in olive oil until creamy in color.

Desserts

Baklava Bites

Growing up, we had close Greek friends, so I ate a lot of baklava and loved it! It is way too sweet for me now, so I substituted brown rice syrup for the honey and it is perfect. It still is sweet and tastes quite authentic.

Ingredients:

Serves 6

2 1/2 cups walnuts, toasted & coarsely chopped
1/2 cup brown rice syrup
1/2 tsp. cinnamon
1 pinch sea salt
safflower oil
1 package pre-made phyllo dough cups

Method:

1. Preheat oven to 350°.
2. Combine walnuts, brown rice syrup, cinnamon, sea salt and 1 tbsp. safflower oil.
3. With a teaspoon measure, scoop nut mixture into phyllo cups.
4. Place on baking sheet, and bake on center rack 5-7 minutes or until golden brown.

You can purchase phyllo dough cups in your grocer's freezer section.

Brown Rice Crispie Squares
with Almonds & Raisins

Who says rice crispie squares can't be healthy? I used to love the marshmallow ones when I was a kid. Now, with a healthy twist, you and your kids will love these too.

Ingredients:

Serves 8-10

4 cups brown rice crispies
1 cup brown rice syrup
1 pinch sea salt
1/2 cup toasted almonds
1/2 cup raisins
2 Tbsps. almond butter
1 tsp. vegetable oil

Method:

1. Gently heat brown rice syrup, salt and oil in a saucepan. After it softens and combines well, add nuts, raisins and nut butter.

2. Put rice crispies in large bowl and add the brown rice syrup mixture. Stir and mix together well.

3. Oil the back of a large spoon and use it to press the rice crispie mixture into a greased 8 x 8 baking dish. Slice into squares before it cools down.

4. Let cool prior to serving.

Add any nut or dried fruit you prefer.

Caramel Corn

Sometimes you want caramel corn, but it's just too sweet. The combination of the barley malt and brown rice syrup gives this treat the right amount of sweetness without the sugar high.

Ingredients:

Serves 4-6

1/2 cup popcorn kernels
1/2 cup brown rice syrup
1-2 Tbsps barley malt
1/4 tsp. cinnamon
sea salt
1/4 cup safflower or vegetable oil
parchment paper

Method:

1. Heat oil in large pot, add popcorn and cover.
2. When popcorn is popped, pour into a colander so un-popped kernels can fall out. Put in a large bowl.
3. Gently heat 1 Tbsp. barley malt, brown rice syrup and cinnamon in a saucepan with a pinch of sea salt until it is smooth and melted. Then taste, if you want a stronger flavor, gradually add the remainder of the barley malt until you achieve the taste you like.
4. Pour syrup mixture onto popcorn and with a spatula, mix until it is thoroughly coated.
5. Let stand 10-15 minutes for it to harden or spread on a parchment-lined cookie sheet and put in a 350° oven for 1 minute.

Cherry Crumble

In the fall, I love to make desserts from the seasonal fruits I buy at the farmer's market. This crumble recipe can be used with any berry or tree fruit. It will warm your soul.

Ingredients:

Serves 4-6

4 cups cherries, pitted
2 Tbsps. kuzu or natural thickening agent
1 tsp. cinnamon
1/4 tsp. sea salt
1/2 cup brown rice syrup
1 tsp. almond extract
1/2 cup water, cold

Topping Ingredients:

1 1/2 cups rolled oats (not instant oatmeal)
1/2 cup whole wheat pastry flour
1/4 cup sliced almonds
1/4 tsp. sea salt
6 Tbsps. vegetable oil
3 Tbsps. brown rice syrup

Method:

1. Preheat oven to 400°.

2. In a small bowl, add the kuzu and cold water. Mix together using your fingers to dissolve kuzu.

3. In a saucepan, add cherries, kuzu mixture, cinnamon and sea salt, Start stirring until white color of kuzu disappears and the cherry liquid starts to thicken.

4. Transfer to either a 1 1/2 or 2 quart baking dish or individual ramekins.

5. To prepare topping, mix dry ingredients together, stir in oil, then brown rice syrup. Rub the mixture between your palms and distribute over fruit.

6. Cover dish with foil, bake until fruit is tender, about 45 minutes or until bubbly. Remove foil and bake until topping is golden brown, approx. 10 minutes.

Dessert Eggrolls

I came up with this recipe when I was teaching a kids' cooking class. The kids really loved them! Use any fruit or nuts you like.

Ingredients:

Serves 8-10

1 cup strawberries, diced
1 1/2 cups walnuts, toasted & coarsely chopped (reserve ½ cup for garnish)
1/2 cup brown rice syrup
1/2 tsp. cinnamon
1 pinch sea salt
1 package eggroll wrappers
safflower oil
paper towels

Method:

1. Combine walnuts, 1/4 cup brown rice syrup, salt and cinnamon. Using a tablespoon, put 1 Tbsp. nut mixture on the diagonal of the eggroll wrapper along with 2 tsps. chopped fruit on top.

2. Wet fingers and moisten edges of eggroll wrapper, fold bottom flap over nut and fruit mixture, then fold sides in, roll up, wet end and seal.

3. Heat 5 inches of oil in Dutch oven and deep-fry until golden brown.

4. Gently heat 1/4 cup brown rice syrup in a saucepan.

5. When eggrolls come out of oil, place on paper towel. Then with a pastry brush, gently brush each eggroll with brown rice syrup.

6. Garnish with walnuts.

Grilled Peaches
with Brown Rice Syrup & Toasted Almonds

Grilling fruit is a great twist for a summer dessert. It really enhances the fruits' flavors and adding toasted almonds gives it a satisfying crunch.

Ingredients:

Serves 2-4

2 peaches, halved & pitted
1/4 cup brown rice syrup
1/2 tsp. cinnamon
1/4 tsp. almond extact
1 cup almonds, toasted & chopped coarsely
olive oil
sea salt

Method:

1. Brush cut-side of peaches with oil and sprinkle with sea salt. Place on hot grill, until there are grill marks, approximately 3 minutes.

2. In a saucepan, gently heat the brown rice syrup, cinnamon and almond extract until it is smooth.

3. When peaches are done, brush a little of the syrup mixture on them and garnish with almonds.

Nut Crunch

If you are craving something sweet and crunchy, this is just the answer. I often make this for holiday treats or thank you gifts. You can use any nuts or seeds you like.

Ingredients:

Serves 6

2 cups almonds, walnuts, peanuts, pumpkin & sunflower seeds
1/2 cup brown rice syrup
1 Tbsp. safflower oil
3/4 tsp. cinnamon
1/4 tsp. allspice
1/2 tsp. ginger
1 tsp. vanilla or almond extract
1 pinch sea salt
1 pinch cayenne powder (optional)
parchment paper

Method:

1. Preheat oven to 350°.
2. Rinse seeds, combine with nuts and dry roast in skillet until lightly browned and fragrant.
3. Gently heat brown rice syrup and spices together. Pour over nuts and seeds in skill and mix thoroughly.
4. Spread nut mixture on a parchment-lined cookie sheet.
5. Bake until syrup bubbles everywhere, approximately 5-10 minutes.
6. Remove from oven and put parchment paper with nut crunch mix onto cooling rack. Let cool to harden, then break into clusters.

Seasonal Fruit Almond Tart

I created this dessert for one of my gluten-free cooking classes. You can use blueberries, raspberries or any seasonal berry, just be prepared for the applause!

Ingredients for Crust:

Serves 6-8

3/4 cup almond flour
3/4 cup walnut flour, (1 cup walnuts processed in food processor)
1/4 tsp. sea salt
1/4 tsp. baking soda
2 Tbsps. safflower oil
2 Tbsps. brown rice or maple syrup

Ingredients for Tart Toppings:

1 small container strawberries, (sliced thin)
1 Tbsp. strawberry jam, warmed gently
1 cup sliced almonds, toasted

Ingredients for Almond Cream Filling:

1 cup almonds
1 cup apple juice
1/2 - 1 cup water
1/2 tsp. almond or vanilla extract
pinch of sea salt
1 Tbsp. brown rice syrup
water

Cream Filling Method:

1 Preheat oven to 350°. Fill water in pot, bring to boil with a pinch of sea salt. Add almonds and blanch 3-4 minutes.

2 Remove almonds from water and rinse with cool water. Remove almond skins by either popping them out with your fingers or rolling them in a kitchen towel.

3 Spread almonds on cookie sheet, bake 10 minutes.

4 Gently warm apple juice, almond or vanilla extract, brown rice syrup and sea salt on a low flame.

5 Pour a little of the juice mixture into the blender, before adding the almonds. Start to blend. Gradually add juice mixture until you achieve a thick cream-like filling consistency. If you need more liquid to reach desired consistency, gradually add water.

6 Refrigerate filling prior to using.

Crust Method:

1 Preheat oven to 350°.

2 In a bowl, mix dry ingredients together, then add wet ingredients and combine together using a fork.

3 Wet fingers and press mixture into a tart or pie pan.

4 Bake 10-15 minutes or until golden brown. Cool before filling.

Tart Topping Method:

1 Spread almond cream filling in crust, arrange fruit on top. With a pastry brush, lightly spread warmed jam onto fruit.

2 Garnish tart with toasted almonds.

Index